100 First Words for Toddlers
유아의 첫 100 단어

English – Korean Bilingual
영어•한국어 동시학습

JAYME YANNUZZI

Translated by **Bora Yu**

Illustrations by **Sarah Rebar**

ROCKRIDGE
PRESS

First Rockridge Press hardcover edition 2022

Originally published in trade paperback by Rockridge Press 2021

For general information on our other products and services, please contact our Customer Care Department within the United States at (866) 744-2665, or outside the United States at (510) 253-0500.

Hardcover ISBN: 979-8-88608-403-0
Paperback ISBN: 978-1-63878-077-9
eBook ISBN: 978-1-63878-317-6

Manufactured in the United States of America

Series Designer: Amanda Kirk
Interior and Cover Designer: Diana Haas
Art Producer: Sara Feinstein
Editor: Laura Bryn Sisson
Production Editor: Nora Milman
Production Manager: Martin Worthington

Illustrations © Sarah Rebar
Illustrator photo courtesy of Jeff Fried

10 9 8 7 6 5 4 3 2 1 0

To my daughter, whose first word, "Mama," was a memory
I will never forget, even if it quickly turned to "duck."
I love you. —J.Y.

내 딸아, 너의 첫 마디가 "엄마" 였다는 걸 결코 안 잊으마, 비록 "오리"로 금방
바뀌긴 했지만…. 사랑한다, 얘야. —J.Y.

To my world – Logan, Remy and the rest of the fam. —B.Y.

나의 온 세상인 사랑하는 로건, 레미, 그리고 우리 가족들에게. —B.Y.

Dear Reader,

Hearing your toddler learn their first words are some of the most special memories you can make together! The best way for your child to learn is by interacting with you, so here are a few tips for how to use this book:

- Point to a picture on the page, say the word, and use it in a sentence.

- Ask questions about what your child notices on each page. You can say, "What are you pointing to?" "What do you see?"

- Play a game of *I Spy*. "I spy with my little eye . . . something yellow. Yes, a duck!"

- Have your toddler collect items around the house to match to the pictures in the book.

Use this book to read, talk, and play with your toddler over and over again.

독자님께,

아기가 말을 배우기 시작하면 부모에게는 소중한 기억들이 더 많이 생겨납니다!
아이는 부모와의 소통을 통해 가장 잘 배울 수 있다는 걸 기억하세요. 이 책을 교재로 쓰실 때 다음을 참고하시면 도움이 될 것입니다.

- 그림을 가리키면서 해당되는 단어를 소리내어 읽어주세요. 이어서, 그 단어를 넣어 문장을 만들어보세요.

- 아이가 각 페이지에서 무엇을 인지하는지 물어보세요. "뭘 가리키는 거니?", "여기 뭐가 보이니?" 등의 질문을 해보세요.

- 아이와 "~가 보인다" 게임을 해 보세요. 예: "내 작은 눈에... 노랑색의 뭔가가 보인다... 맞아, 오리다!"

- 아이한테 책에 나온 그림과 일치하는 물건이나 장난감을 집 안팎에서 찾아보도록 하는 것도 좋은 방법입니다.

이 책을 활용하면서 계속해서 읽고, 말하며, 아이와 놀아 주세요.

airplane
비행기
(bee-haeng-ghi)

apple
사과
(sah-gwah)

baby
아기
(ah-ghi)

ball
공
(gohng)

balloon
풍선
(poong-sun)

banana
바나나
(bah-nah-nah)

bath
목욕
(moh-gyok)

bed
침대
(chim-dae)

belly
배
(bae)

bib
턱받이
(tuck-bbah-gee)

bird
새
(sae)

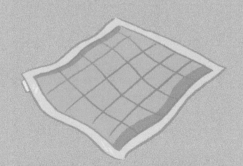

blanket
담요
(dahm-yo)

blocks
블록
(bul-lok)

boat
배
(bae)

book
책
(chaek)

bookshelf
책장
(chaek-jahng)

bottle
젖병
(jut-byung)

bowl
그릇
(gu-rute)

bubbles
거품
(guh-poom)

bug
벌레
(buhl-leh)

bunny
토끼
(toh-kkee)

car
자동차
(jah-dong-chah)

carrot
당근
(dahng-gune)

cat
고양이
(goh-yahng-ee)

cereal
시리얼
(shi-ree-uhl)

chair
의자
(ui-jah)

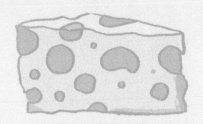

cheese
치즈
(chee-ju)

chicken
닭
(dahk)

circle
동그라미
(dong-gu-rah-mee)

closet
옷장
(oht-jahng)

coat
외투
(weh-too)

cookie
쿠키
(coo-kee)

couch
소파
(soh-pah)

cow
소
(soh)

crayon
크레용
(ku-reh-yong)

cup
컵
(cup)

diaper
기저귀
(ghi-juh-gwi)

dog
개
(gae)

doll
인형
(in-hyung)

door
문
(moon)

drawer
서랍
(suh-rahp)

drink
마시다
(mah-shi-dah)

duck
오리
(oh-ree)

ears
귀
(gwi)

eat
먹다
(muck-dah)

eyes
눈
(noon)

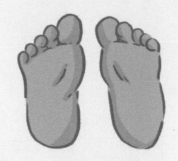

feet
발
(bahl)

flower
꽃
(ggoht)

fork
포크
(poh-ku)

grass
풀
(pool)

happy
행복하다
(hang-bok-kah-dah)

hat
모자
(moh-jah)

head
머리
(muh-ree)

heart
하트
(hah-tu)

house
집
(jip)

juice
주스
(joo-su)

keys
열쇠
(yuhl-sweh)

lamp
램프
(lamb-pu)

lion
사자
(sah-jah)

milk
우유
(ooh-yoo)

monkey
원숭이
(won-soong-ee)

mouth
입
(ip)

neck
목
(mohk)

noodles
국수
(gook-soo)

nose
코
(koh)

pants
바지
(bah-jee)

paper
종이
(johng-ee)

park
공원
(gohng-won)

peas
완두콩
(wan-doo-kong)

pig
돼지
(dweh-jee)

pillow
베개
(beh-gae)

plate
접시
(juhp-shi)

play
놀다
(nohl-dah)

potty
변기
(byun-ghi)

sad
슬프다
(sul-pu-dah)

shirt
셔츠
(shiuh-chu)

shoe
신발
(shin-bahl)

shorts
반바지
(bahn-bah-jee)

sleep
자다
(jah-dah)

slide
미끄럼틀
(me-ggu-rum-tul)

socks
양말
(yahng-mahl)

spoon
숟가락
(soot-gah-rahk)

square
네모
(neh-moh)

stairs
계단
(gyeh-dahn)

star
별
(byul)

strawberry
딸기
(ddahl-ghi)

stroller
유모차
(yoo-moh-cha)

swing
그네
(gu-neh)

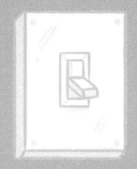

switch
스위치
(su-we-chi)

table
탁자
(tahk-jah)

teddy bear
곰 인형
(goh-min-hyung)

towel
수건
(soo-gun)

train
기차
(ghi-cha)

tree
나무
(nah-moo)

triangle
세모
(seh-moh)

truck
트럭
(tu-ruck)

umbrella
우산
(ooh-sahn)

wagon
수레
(soo-reh)

walk
걷다
(gut-dah)

window
창문
(chahng-moon)

About the Author

Jayme Yannuzzi, M. Elementary Ed., is a former first grade teacher and the creator of the blog *Teach Talk Inspire*, where she shares resources to entertain and educate kids at home.

About the Illustrator

Sarah Rebar is an illustrator based in Los Angeles, with a BFA in Illustration and Design from Syracuse University. She loves to draw stories and fun illustrations for kids.

About the Translator

Bora Yu is a reformed financial services professional turned stay-at-home mom of two. She has an affinity for all things food, language, and culture. Her first love will always be Korean.

Printed in the USA
CPSIA information can be obtained
at www.ICGtesting.com
CBHW040848230424
6611CB00006B/8